DELAWARE PATRIOTS

Their Lives, Contributions, and Burial Sites

JOE FARRELL • LAWRENCE KNORR • JOE FARLEY

SUNBURY PRESS

Mechanicsburg, PA USA

Published by Sunbury Press, Inc.
Mechanicsburg, Pennsylvania

SUNBURY
P R E S S
www.sunburypress.com

For information about special discounts for bulk purchases, please contact Sunbury Press Orders Dept. at (855) 338-8359 or orders@sunburypress.com.

To request one of our authors for speaking engagements or book signings, please contact Sunbury Press Publicity Dept. at publicity@sunburypress.com.

FIRST SUNBURY PRESS EDITION: February 2025

Set in Adobe Garamond | Interior design by Crystal Devine | Cover by Lawrence Knorr | Edited by the authors.

Publisher's Cataloging-in-Publication Data
Names: Farrell, Joe, author | Farley, Joe, author | Knorr, Lawrence, author.
Title: Delaware patriots : their lives, contributions, and burial sites / Joe Farrell Lawrence Knorr Joe Farley.
Description: First trade paperback edition. | Mechanicsburg, PA : Sunbury Press, 2025.
Summary: The individuals from Delaware who played prominent roles in the founding of the USA are detailed.
Identifiers: ISBN 979-8-88819-296-2 (softcover).
Subjects: HISTORY / United States / Revolutionary Period (1775-1800) | BIOGRAPHY & AUTOBIOGRAPHY / Political.

Designed in the USA
0 1 1 2 3 5 8 13 21 34 55

For the Love of Books!

Contents

Introduction

Welcome to *Delaware Patriots*. This work aims to examine the lives and contributions of the amazing men and women who using their courage and talents, established the country those of us who live here, and many who do not have come to love. Our original plan called for a four-volume series, with each covering approximately fifty Founders, and that goal remains. However, based on our research, we have found that adding volumes that examine specific states is beneficial. As a result, we published a volume titled *Pennsylvania Patriots* in 2019, and this volume encompasses patriots buried in Delaware. Other state books will follow.

Over the past decade, we have made trips to numerous cemeteries to produce twelve volumes of the popular Keystone Tombstones and two titled Gotham Graves. This series covering the Founders follows the same format of those works and involved more effort in both time and research. Our travels to visit the graves of those we have identified as Founders have taken us to more than the thirteen original states. Accessing information about some of the lesser-known individuals who made contributions to the creation of the United States at times has been challenging. We hope that our efforts in meeting those challenges will please our readers.

The first question we had to answer regarding this series was who to include. In other words, who qualifies to be considered a founder? The standard we settled on resulted in the inclusion of signers of either the Continental Association, the Declaration of Independence, the Articles of Confederation, or the Constitution. In addition, we have also identified non-signers of the above-referenced documents who made significant contributions to the creation of the United States of America. John Paul Jones is an example of the latter group.

We all agree that our visits to the gravesites and the research on the Founders have been rewarding and educational. However, in some cases, the visits have been sobering, shocking, and shameful. The well-known Founders such as Washington, Jefferson, Hamilton, and Madison have been laid to rest in well-maintained graves accessible to the public. Unfortunately, this is not the rule. Too many of our nation's Founders are buried in neglected places and have been left unattended and thus are subject to decay. Some are inaccessible, and others cannot be located at all due to the development of the land and poor record keeping. One of our goals in doing this series and including photographs of the graves is to bring this problem to light and hopefully spurn action to address this issue before it is simply too late.

Considering the condition of many of these graves, we have established a website, www.adoptapatriot.com, where one can find information on all the people we have identified as Founders. We continue to update this site as we come across new information. In addition, the website includes a Wall of Shame where we highlight those gravesites that we have concluded are in the worst shape due to neglect or are in remote difficult to reach locations or where the founder is under memorialized given their contributions to the nation. It is our sincere hope that many of these graves will be restored, renewed, or relocated.

One thing we have learned about the Founders in writing this series, and we are confident that most of them would agree with us, is that they were products of their times and not perfect nor infallible. They disagreed on many of the issues they faced, and none may have been as hotly debated as slavery. As a matter of fact, on our many trips, we have had some heated debates as to how the various Founders dealt with slavery on both public and personal levels. It is difficult to reconcile men who undertook a war against the most powerful army in the world, proclaiming that all men are created equal while, at the same time, many of these same men held other men, women, and children in bondage. The contradiction is obvious and quite difficult to excuse. Nevertheless, we have attempted to tell each founder's story truthfully and deal with the slavery issue on a case-by-case basis.

As the country nears the upcoming 250th anniversary of the Declaration of Independence, we view these volumes as timely reminders of the Founders' sacrifices and contributions to create this nation. We should never forget those who put their lives and fortunes on the line and succeeded in establishing the greatest country the world has ever known. We are inspired by the words of Marcus Cicero:

POOR IS THE NATION HAVING NO HEROES
SHAMEFUL THE ONE THAT HAVING THEM FORGETS

John Dickinson
(1732–1808)

Penman of the Revolution

Buried at Friends Meeting House Burial Grounds,
Wilmington, Delaware.

Thought Leader • Military • Articles of Confederation
U.S. Constitution

This founder favored reconciliation with the mother country as opposed to declaring American Independence. As a delegate from Pennsylvania to the Continental Congress, he abstained on the vote for independence. He also declined to sign the document that declared it. After his fellow delegates passed that motion, he left Congress and joined the Continental Army and fought in the Revolution. Despite not favoring independence he had worked with Thomas Jefferson on a document titled *A Declaration of the Causes and Necessity of Taking Up Arms*. He also authored *Letters from a Farmer in Pennsylvania* in which he argued that the English Parliament did not have the authority to tax the colonies. These writings earned him the title "Penman of the Revolution." Thus his writings were seen to have ignited the fires for a cause that he refused to endorse. During his life, he served as the president of two states Pennsylvania and Delaware, and he represented the latter at the 1787 Constitutional Convention. His signature is also affixed to the document produced by that gathering. Thomas Jefferson called him a true patriot, and he was undoubtedly a man known to stand by his principles regardless of the cost. His name was John Dickinson.

John Dickinson

Dickinson was born on or around November 8, 1732, on his family's tobacco plantation, which was located in Maryland. His father had inherited the estate of 2,500 acres which he expanded to 9,000 acres. He also purchased land in Delaware where he started another plantation and christened it Poplar Hall. These were profitable ventures that were worked using slave labor until 1777 when the subject of this chapter freed the slaves of Poplar Hall.

In his youth, Dickinson was educated at his home by tutors. The most important of these was William Killen, who became the lifelong friend of his student. Killen himself would become Delaware's first Chief Justice and Chancellor. At the age of 18, Dickinson began the study of law under John Milan in Philadelphia. He also spent three years in England to continue those studies before being admitted to the Pennsylvania Bar in 1757.

By 1770 Dickinson was a successful lawyer and one of the wealthiest men in the colonies. That year he married Mary "Polly" Norris whose father was the Speaker of the Pennsylvania General Assembly. Dickinson's wife would inherit 500 acres in Carlisle, Pennsylvania that the couple would donate to John and Mary's College in 1784. The College was re-named Dickinson College. Thus he was bestowed the honor of having an institution of higher learning named in his honor while he still walked the earth.

The Norris family were Quakers as the Dickinson's had been un-til a dispute with the sect over a family marriage led to a break with the Quaker society. Though Dickinson himself never became an active Quaker, he believed in many Quaker principles though not pacifism since he did not object to a defensive war. It was this belief that allowed him to join the Continental Army and fight in defense of the newly formed United States.

After his wedding, Dickinson's political career blossomed. It was during this period that he enhanced his reputation throughout the colonies through his writings, as mentioned earlier, that were critical of the English Parliament's imposition of the Townshend Acts. Dickinson wrote that while the English government could regulate commerce, they had no authority to tax. He warned his fellow citizens that accepting the Townshend Acts would result in other taxes being levied on the colonies in the future.

In 1774 Dickinson was selected to represent Pennsylvania in the Continental Congress. It was here that he urged his fellow delegates to pursue a peaceful solution with England. It was his view that inde-pendence was not in the best interests of the colonies. His arguments failed to convince Congress, and when the vote was conducted on July 2, 1776, to declare independence, he abstained. He felt that standing by his convictions would be detrimental to his political future. He said, "My conduct this day, I expect will give the finishing blow to my once too great and, my integrity considered, now too diminished popularity."

Though he refused to sign the declaration, during his lifetime, Dickinson was recognized as a significant influence on the subject based on his previous writings. As a matter of fact, in 1787, Thomas Jefferson read an article in the *Journal de Paris* that put forth the position that it was the influence of Dickinson that resulted in the adoption of American independence. Jefferson wrote a long letter to the editor in which he insisted that Dickinson was on the other side of the question and would point out the error in the article himself if given a chance. The author of the declaration never mailed the letter which was discovered among his papers after his death. Some have theorized that Jefferson didn't have the letter delivered because it would appear as self-serving even though he makes clear that its purpose was to correct the historical record.

Leaving Congress, Dickinson accepted a position as a Brigadier General in the Pennsylvania militia. In this position, he commanded 10,000 troops which were dispatched to Elizabeth, New Jersey in anticipation of a British attack. After being passed over by promotions that went to two junior officers, Dickinson resigned his commission and returned to Poplar Hall in Delaware. It was here that he learned that his home in Philadelphia had been confiscated by the British and turned into a hospital. Some believe that Dickinson's failure to support independence resulted in the decision on promotions that prompted his resignation.

It appears that Dickinson's fears that refusing to sign the Declaration would result in a significant loss of public support were unfounded. In 1777 the Delaware General Assembly tried to send him back to the Continental Congress, but he refused to serve. Instead, he served as a private in the Kent County Militia under Caesar Rodney. When his friend Thomas McKean tried to promote him to the post of Brigadier General of the Delaware Militia he again declined to serve in that capacity. It was during this period that Dickinson freed the 37 slaves who worked at Poplar Hall.

In 1779 Dickinson agreed to represent Delaware in the Continental Congress. As a member of this group, he signed the Articles of Confederation which was a document he had worked on as a Pennsylvania delegate in 1776. He left Congress in 1781 after learning that a loyalist raid had severely damaged Poplar Hall. Back in Kent County, he was elected to represent that area in the State Senate. Shortly after taking his seat the General Assembly elected him to the office of President of Delaware. Less than a year later he was also elected to the Supreme Executive Council of Pennsylvania. When the Pennsylvania General Assembly elected him president of the council, he became the State President of both Delaware and Pennsylvania simultaneously.

In 1787 Dickinson was among Delaware's representatives at the Constitutional Convention. He played an essential role there. Dickinson

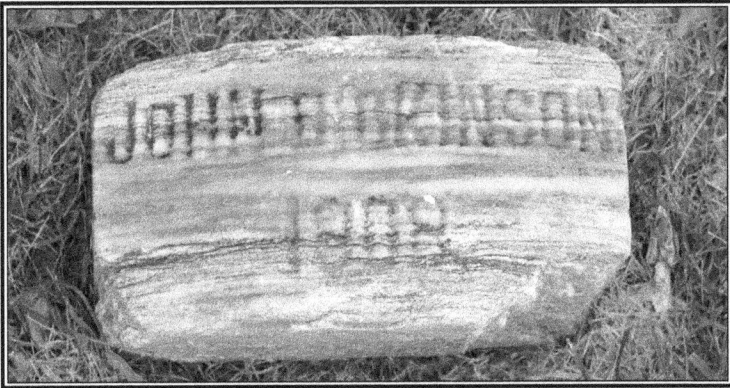

The modest grave of John Dickinson

aided in the development of the Great Compromise which resulted in seats in the House of Representatives being based on population while each state received two seats in the United States Senate. Sick and ailing as the Convention reached its end he returned to Delaware but directed George Read to affix his name to the Constitution. Though he had opportunities to serve in the government established by the Constitution, Dickinson declined. Some believe he made this decision because he had experienced enough of the strains of public life in the years between the Stamp Act Congress and the Constitutional Convention. He left the world of politics entirely in 1793 after serving a final term in the Delaware Senate.

Dickinson lived until 1808. He spent the final 15 years of his life working on the abolition of slavery while making significant donations to organizations working in Dickinson's words to the "relief of the unhappy." He passed away at the age of 75 and was laid to rest in the Friends Meeting House Burial Ground located in Wilmington, Delaware. Responding to Dickinson's passing, Thomas Jefferson wrote, "A more estimable man, or a truer patriot, could not have left us. Among the first of the advocates for the rights of his country when assailed by Great Britain, he continued to the last the orthodox advocate of the true principles of our new government and his name will be consecrated in history as one of the worthies of the Revolution."

Richard Bassett
(1745–1815)

Senator #1

Buried at Wilmington & Brandywine Cemetery,
Wilmington, Delaware

U.S. Constitution

Richard Bassett, a native of Delaware, was an attorney, politician, Revolutionary War soldier, signer of the U.S. Constitution, U.S. senator, Chief Justice of the Court of Common Pleas, governor, and a United States circuit judge. According to Senate records, he is ranked as senator #1 in United States history.

Richard Bassett was born April 2, 1745, in Cecil County, Maryland, the son of Arnold Bassett, a farmer and tavern-keeper, and his wife, Judith (née Thompson) Bassett. After being abandoned by his father, Bassett was raised by Peter Lawson, a relative of his mother, from whom he later inherited his Bohemia Manor estate.

Bassett attended preparatory schools and then pursued a career in the law, studying in Philadelphia. He was admitted to the Delaware bar in 1770 and practiced law in Kent County, near Dover. He also prospered as a planter and eventually came to own Bohemia Manor and homes in Dover and Wilmington. Focusing on religious and charitable pursuits, he rose among the local gentry and was known for his hospitality and philanthropy.

Bassett married twice, first to Mary Ennals and second to Betsy Garnett. He fathered several children, including Anne "Nancy" Bassett, who later married James Asheton Bayard II. Bassett was a devout

Methodist, held religious meetings at Bohemia Manor, and supported the church financially.

A natural politician, Bassett was elected by his fellow citizens of Kent County in 1774 to serve on the Boston Relief Committee. This group sought to collect contributions for those suffering from the hardships of the Coercive Acts passed by Parliament. Bassett soon found himself in the company of Caesar Rodney, his brother Thomas, and John Haslet, who would command Delaware's regiment in the Continental Army. Bassett served on the Kent County Council of Safety and was a member of the state constitutional convention in 1776. He was also a state senator and representative.

Bassett was integrally involved with military affairs, planning the mobilization in Delaware. He helped to organize Haslet's regiment and selected officers based on merit. Haslet's regiment was later judged among the best under Washington's command. Bassett was also effective in raising troops for Washington's Flying Camp and helped organize Captain Thomas Rodney's Dover Light Infantry, which saw action in the Trenton-Princeton campaign late in 1776. When the British entered the Chesapeake Bay in the summer of 1777 with their sights on Philadelphia, Bassett volunteered for service and joined General Caesar Rodney to delay the British advance. After the British left Philadelphia, Bassett returned to Kent County, where he assumed command of the Dover Light Horse cavalry unit.

The service in the military hardened Bassett, who became more serious and direct as a leader rather than the affable socialite. He filled several political roles, including as a member of the Delaware Legislative Council in 1782 and the Delaware House of Representatives in 1786. Also, that year he represented Delaware at the Annapolis Convention.

The following year, he was a delegate to the Constitutional Convention. Though a relatively quiet delegate, Bassett strongly supported the Great Compromise designed to protect the rights of the small states. It called for a national legislature that gave an equal voice to all thirteen states in a Senate composed of two senators from each but based representation in a House of Representatives on population. Bassett signed the U.S. Constitution and was then a key member of the Delaware ratifying convention making Delaware the first state.

Bassett returned to his law practice in Wilmington from 1787 to 1789, at which point he was elected as a U.S. senator on March 4, 1789, serving until March 3, 1793. Among the first U.S. senators, he is listed as the first U.S. senator on the seniority ranking due to being first alphabetically. In the Senate, Bassett was allied with the moderate wing of the Federalist party being organized by Vice President John Adams. In that capacity, he voted in favor of the president's power to remove governmental officers and against Hamilton's plan for the federal assumption of state debts. Reflecting the continuing concerns of the small states, Bassett was the first to vote for locating the new national capital away from New York and Pennsylvania in an independent federal district on the banks of the Potomac River.

Bassett was a member of the Delaware state constitutional convention in 1792, playing a principal role, along with John Dickinson, in drafting a new constitution for Delaware.

From 1793 to 1799, Bassett served as the first chief justice of Delaware's court of common pleas. In 1796 he served as a member of the Electoral College in the presidential election, casting his votes for John Adams.

From 1799 to 1801, Bassett served as the fourth governor of Delaware. His focus was on the revitalization of the Delaware militia and worked to establish a continental army.

On February 18, 1801, President John Adams nominated Bassett to the U.S. Circuit Court through one of his "midnight appointments." He was confirmed by the U.S. Senate on February 20 and served until the court was abolished on July 1, 1802, by Jeffersonian Republicans.

Bassett spent the rest of his life on his plantation known as Bohemia Manor in Cecil County, Maryland. He died there on September 15, 1815. Said Reverend Henry Boehm of the place,

> This mansion, let it be remarked, which was distinguished for its antiquity, for the splendid paintings that adorned its walls, for the hospitality that reigned there, and as the home of Bishop Asbury when he preached on Bohemia Manor, was burned down many years ago.

Bassett was initially interred in a vault at Bohemia Manor in Cecil County, Maryland. An elaborate funeral was held at the estate, but no religious services were performed at the vault due to the large turnout. Some years later, after the fire, the vault was broken into, and the graves disturbed. In 1865, Bassett's remains were moved to Wilmington and Brandywine Cemetery in Wilmington, Delaware.

Recalled his friend, Reverend Henry Boehm,

> . . . at one time, Governor Bassett was a very fashionable man, and being rich, had his good things in this life. But after his conversion, he was as humble and teachable as a little child. At this remote period, it is impossible to have a correct idea of the position he once occupied and the influence he exerted in favor of the church of his choice, in whose annals he should ever have a prominent place.
>
> In person, Governor Bassett was a stout-built man of medium height and looked as if he was made for service. His countenance was full of benignity, his eye was very expressive, and his voice

The tomb containing the body of Richard Bassett

strong and musical. He was distinguished for benevolence and was given to hospitality. He had three homes, residing part of the time in Dover, then on Bohemia Manor, and then in Wilmington. He has entertained over one hundred persons at one time. His heart was as large as his mansion.

Bassett was the grandfather of U.S. Senators from Delaware; Richard H. Bayard and James A. Bayard Jr. Bassett Street in Madison, Wisconsin, is named after him.

Gunning Bedford Jr.
(1747–1812)

Constitution Signer from Delaware

Buried at Wilmington – Brandywine Cemetery,
Wilmington Delaware.

Continental Congress • U.S. Constitution

Gunning Bedford Jr. was an American lawyer and politician from Wilmington, Delaware, who served in the state legislature and the Continental Army before being elected to the Continental Congress. He was a delegate to the U.S. Constitutional Convention and signed the famous document at its conclusion. He was a delegate to the Delaware Ratification Convention, where he urged ratification. Delaware was the first to do so.

Gunning Bedford was born in Philadelphia on April 13, 1747. He was the fifth of seven children and one of nine Gunning Bedfords in the family. They numbered his grandfather, father, son, three cousins, two second cousins, and a third cousin. He always used Jr. to distinguish himself among them. He left there at age 20 to attend the College of New Jersey, which is now Princeton University and where he was a classmate of James Madison. He graduated with honors in 1771. He married Jane Ballareau Parker, and sources differ on how many children they had.

He studied law with Joseph Read in New York and eventually gained admission to the bar and set up practice in Dover and Wilmington, Delaware. He served in the Continental Army during these years and,

Gunning Bedford Jr.

in July 1775, was elected to serve as Deputy Muster General for New York. In June 1776, he was promoted to Muster Master General for New York. Other than that, little is known about his Revolutionary War activities.

He began his career in elective politics in 1783 when he was elected to the Delaware House of Representatives for the first of four terms and then one three-year term (1788–1791) in the State Senate. In 1784 he was appointed Delaware's first Attorney General. He held that position for five years.

Bedford also served in the Continental Congress from 1783–1785. In 1786 he was selected to represent his state at the Annapolis Convention but did not attend the sessions. Attendance was very low at Annapolis, and it failed to achieve its goals, but it led to a call for what became the Constitutional Convention.

The government that had been established under the Articles of Confederation was floundering by 1786. Bedford and George Read, Jacob Broom, John Dickinson, and Richard Bassett were appointed a commissioner to meet in Philadelphia for what was to become one of the most important events in our nation's history—the United States Constitutional Convention.

Bedford arrived on May 28, 1787, and regularly attended its sessions. He was a large and forceful man and spoke often. He was concerned primarily with the fate of the small states in a federal union potentially dominated by powerful populous neighbors. He warned the delegates in Philadelphia in a speech on June 30 that the small states might have to seek foreign alliances for their protection. The idea was shouted down as treasonous and threw the convention into turmoil. At first, he joined with those who sought to merely amend the Articles of Confederation, but when the idea of drafting a new Constitution was accepted, he became more flexible and supported what was known as the New Jersey Plan. This plan provided equal representation for the states in the national legislature, a point on which the Delaware legislature had instructed its delegates not to compromise.

In early July, a compromise committee was formed by Benjamin Franklin, and Bedford was appointed a member. This committee recommended that in the second branch of congress, each state should have an equal vote. On July 16, when a vote was taken, the great compromise was adopted by a 5-4 vote.

Bedford returned to Delaware and was a delegate to Delaware's Ratification Convention in 1787. He used his experience and eloquence to encourage early ratification. He and Richard Bassett signed both the Constitution and Delaware's ratification document. Delaware became the first state to approve the Constitution.

In 1789 and again in 1793, Bedford served as a presidential elector and cast his vote both times for George Washington. On September 24, 1789, he was nominated by President George Washington to be the first

The grave of Gunning Bedford Jr.

judge for the United States District Court for the District of Delaware. He was confirmed by the Senate on September 26 and received his commission the same day. He resigned as Delaware's Attorney General and held the District Judge position until his death.

Bedford never lost interest in his local community, and he worked for the improvement of education in Wilmington. He served as president of the Board of Trustees of Wilmington Academy, and when that institution became Wilmington College, he became its first president.

On March 30, 1812, he died at Wilmington at the age of 65 and was buried first in the Presbyterian cemetery there. Later, when the cemetery was abandoned, his body was transferred to the Masonic Home Cemetery in Christiana, Delaware. In 2013, after the sale of the Masonic Home, his monument, Bedford, and the remains of his family were relocated to the historic Wilmington-Brandywine Cemetery in Wilmington. His grave is marked with a large beautiful, bullet-shaped monument.

Gunning Bedford Jr. (1747–1812)

The monument lists his major accomplishments and then reads, "He so behaved in these high offices as to deserve and receive the approbation of his fellow citizens. His form was goodly, his temper amiable, his manner winning, and his discharge of private duties exemplary. Reader, may his example stimulate you to improve the talents—be they five or two, or one—with which God has entrusted you."

Thomas McKean
(1735–1817)

"First Elected President of the Confederation"

Buried at Laurel Hill Cemetery,
Philadelphia, Pennsylvania

**Military • Declaration of Independence
Articles of Confederation**

This founder was known for his very brusque take-charge attitude that at times upset his fellow patriots. This may have contributed to the fact that while serving in the Stamp Act Congress, two other delegates challenged him to duels which he speedily accepted. Only the departure of one representative and the existence of cooler heads avoided the shedding of blood. His resume is lengthy and in addition to service in Congress included service in the military. He also served as Governor of Delaware and as Chief Justice of Pennsylvania at the same time. He would later attend the Pennsylvania convention that ratified the United States Constitution and serve as the Governor of that state. He also affixed his signature to both the Declaration of Independence and the Articles of Confederation. Some contend that he served as one of the first Presidents of the United States under those Articles. His name was Thomas McKean.

McKean was born on March 19, 1734, in New London Township located in Chester County, Pennsylvania. His parents were both Irish born Ulster-Scots who came to America from Ballymoney, County

Thomas McKean (1735–1817)

Thomas McKean

Antrim, Ireland. When McKean was 16 years of age, he traveled to New Castle, Delaware to study the law under one of his cousins. By 1756 he had been admitted to the bar in both Delaware and Pennsylvania. By the mid-1760s he was serving in the Delaware General Assembly and as a judge of the Court of Common Pleas. Delaware at the time had two political factions which were commonly referred to as the "Court Party" and the "Country Party." The former party urged reconciliation with England while the latter, of which McKean was a leading member, supported American independence.

In 1765, Mckean and Caesar Rodney represented Delaware at the Stamp Act Congress. McKean was an active member of this group and along with John Rutledge and Philip Livingston served on the committee that drafted the Declaration of Rights and Grievances. Timothy Ruggles,

a delegate from Massachusetts who served as president of the body, refused to sign the Memorial. Ruggles also declined to state the reasons
for his objection. McKean wouldn't let the matter drop and demanded
that Ruggles explain himself. The Massachusetts delegate then explained
that his conscience would not permit him to address complaints to
the king. McKean responded with scorn twice bellowing out the word
conscience in a sarcastic manner that Ruggles viewed as an insult. He
challenged McKean to a duel which was immediately accepted. Early
the next morning Ruggles returned to his home state, so no duel was
fought. The Massachusetts legislature officially censured Ruggles for "a
neglect of duty." Ruggles wasn't the only delegate at the gathering to
draw McKean's ire. Robert Ogden, a representative from New Jersey, also
challenged McKean to a meeting on the field of honor. McKean accepted
this invitation but cooler heads in attendance interceded, and the quarrel
was settled without a shot being fired.

McKean would marry twice and father eleven children. His first wife,
Mary Borden, passed away in 1773. A year later he married Sarah Armitage
and moved his family to Philadelphia. Despite his Pennsylvania residence
he was elected to represent Delaware in the Continental Congress. As a
member of Congress, McKean is remembered for the part he played in
fellow delegate Caesar Rodney's midnight ride. On July 1, 1776, McKean
concluded that another delegate from Delaware, George Read, intended
to vote against declaring American independence. Rodney, who like
McKean favored independence, was absent from Congress due to a severe illness. Realizing that Rodney's vote would be needed McKean sent a
messenger to Rodney who had returned to his home in Dover, Delaware.
The message urged his fellow delegate to return to Philadelphia at once.
Rodney immediately mounted a horse and began the eighty-mile trip
back to Congress. As McKean later remembered in a letter to one of
Rodney's nephews, he met Rodney "at the State-house door in his boots
and spurs as the members were assembling; after a friendly salutation
(without a word on the business) we went into the Hall of Congress
together, and found we were among the latest: proceedings immediately
commenced, and after a few minutes the great question was put; when
the vote for Delaware was called, your uncle arose and said: 'As I believe

the voice of my constituents and of all the sensible & honest men is in favor of Independence & my own judgment concurs with them I vote for Independence." Read voted nay but by a margin of two to one Delaware favored independence.

McKean did not get to sign the Declaration of Independence with his fellow members of Congress. Soon after casting his vote he led a militia group to assist George Washington during the unsuccessful defense of New York City. As a result of this military duty, McKean is considered to be the last signer of the Declaration of Independence. McKean insisted that he signed the document sometime in 1776 though most historians believe he affixed his signature to the document between 1777 and 1781.

The war years weren't quiet ones for McKean. He had been placed on the English hit list and wrote in a letter to John Adams that "he was being hunted like a fox." When the British captured the rebel governor of Delaware, McKean assumed the post. At the same time he was serving quite capably as Chief Justice of Pennsylvania in a post he filled from 1777 until 1799. According to his biographer John Coleman, "only the historiographical difficultly of reviewing court records and other scattered documents prevents recognition that McKean, rather than John Marshall, did more than anyone else to establish an independent judiciary in the United States. As Chief Justice under a Pennsylvania constitution he considered flawed, he assumed it the right of the court to strike down legislative acts it deemed unconstitutional, preceding by ten years the U.S. Supreme Court's establishment of the doctrine of judicial review."

In October of 1776 the during what was viewed as a conservative reaction against independence, the Delaware General Assembly did not re-elect McKean to the newly declared nation's Congress. Within a year British occupation of the state changed public opinion, and McKean was returned to Congress in 1777. He would serve in this body until 1783. He helped draft the Articles of Confederation and voted for their adoption in 1781. That same year he was elected to the position of President of Congress. Though primarily a ceremonial position with little authority some have argued that McKean served as President of the United States.

Though he did not attend the Constitutional Convention, McKean took a leading role in securing Pennsylvania's ratification of the United

The grave of Thomas McKean.

States Constitution. He argued in favor of a strong executive and was a member of the state convention that voted to ratify the document. When American political parties came into being, he allied himself initially with the Federalists. By the mid-1790s he broke with that party because of disagreements with compromises that the administration in Philadelphia made with Great Britain. He became an outspoken Jeffersonian Republican.

In 1799 McKean was elected to the first of three terms he would serve as Governor of Pennsylvania. As Governor, he demanded that things be done his way. He removed his critics from government posts and rewarded his supporters with jobs. His administration was so stormy that he had to survive an impeachment attempt by his political foes in 1807. In this, he proved successful.

McKean passed away in 1817 at the age of 83. He was initially laid to rest in the First Presbyterian Church Cemetery, but his remains were moved to Philadelphia's Laurel Hill Cemetery in 1843. In a letter to one of McKean's sons, John Adams described his fellow founder as "among the best tried and firmest pillars of the Revolution."

McKean County, Pennsylvania is named in his honor. There is also a McKean Street in Philadelphia. Both the University of Delaware and Penn State University have buildings named for him.

George Read
(1733–1798)

Triple Signer

Buried at Immanuel Episcopal Churchyard,
New Castle, Delaware

**Continental Association • Declaration of Independence
U.S. Constitution**

George Read was a highly active member of the Continental Congress from Delaware during the Revolutionary period. A politician from New Castle, he signed the Continental Association, Declaration of Independence, and the U.S. Constitution, one of only three statesmen to have signed all three documents. Read also served as President of Delaware, US Senator from Delaware, and the Chief Justice of Delaware.

George Read was born September 18, 1733, in Cecil County, Maryland, the son and eldest of eight children of John Read, an Irish immigrant, and his wife, Mary (née Howell) Read. The elder Read was born in Dublin, Ireland, the son of a wealthy Englishman from Berkshire, Hertfordshire, and Oxfordshire. He came to Maryland and Delaware to seek his fortune after his father's death, purchased a large estate in Cecil County, Maryland, and founded Charlestown with six associates. The goal was to establish a rival market to Baltimore further south and establish the Principio Company, an ironworks. The Washingtons were also interested in this venture. For many years, John Read was a member of the Maryland colonial legislature, held military offices, and later retired to his plantation in New Castle County, Delaware.

George Read

Soon after George Read was born, the family moved to New Castle, Delaware, settling near the village of Christiana. Read attended school at the Reverend Francis Allison's Academy in New London, Pennsylvania, along with Thomas McKean. He then studied law with John Moland and was admitted to the Pennsylvania Bar in 1753. The next year, he returned to New Castle and opened a law practice.

In 1763, Read married Gertrude Ross Till, the daughter of the Reverend George Ross, the rector of the Immanuel Church in New Castle. She was also the widowed sister of George Ross, a future signer of the Declaration of Independence. Together, they had four children, John, George Jr., William, and Mary. The couple lived on The Strand in New Castle. Their home is presently now the Read House and Gardens managed by the Delaware Historical Society is a restoration built by the son following an 1824 fire. Read was later described by a descendant as "tall, slightly and gracefully formed, with pleasing features and lustrous brown eyes. His manners were dignified, bordering upon austerity, but courteous, and at times captivating. He commanded entire confidence, not only from his profound legal knowledge, sound judgment, and impartial decisions but from his severe integrity and the purity of his private character."

At this time, colonial governor John Penn appointed Read the Crown Attorney General for three Delaware counties, succeeding John Ross. He served in this position until 1774. He also served in the Colonial Assembly of the Lower Counties for twelve sessions.

Read was very outspoken from the start regarding the difficulties with Britain. He spoke out against the Boston Port Bill and, along with McKean, Dickinson, and others, led Delaware against the crown. Read was appointed to the First Continental Congress in 1774. While he signed the Continental Association, he was not an early advocate for outright independence. Instead, he was a signer of the Olive Branch Petition, seeking reconciliation with the king. When Congress voted for independence on July 2, 1776, Read voted against it. This prompted the need for Ceasar Rodney to quickly ride to Philadelphia to flip Delaware in favor. However, when it came time to sign the document, Read was there with his pen.

Explaining Read's thinking at the time, historian Charles Goodrich wrote in 1842, "It has already been noticed that when the great question of independence came before Congress, Mr. Read was opposed to the measure, and ultimately gave his vote against it. This he did from a sense of duty: not that he was unfriendly to the liberties of his country or was actuated by motives of selfishness or cowardice. But he deemed the agitation of the question, at the time premature and inexpedient. In these sentiments, Mr. Read was not alone. Many gentlemen in the colonies, characterized for great wisdom, and a decided patriotism, deemed the measure impolitic and would have voted had they been in Congress, as he did. The idle bodings of these, fortunately, were never realized." Read changed his vote after Romney arrived to make Delaware unanimous.

Following independence, Delaware elected Read its Speaker of the Legislative Council of the Delaware General Assembly, effectively the governor. He, with the assistance of Thomas McKean, drafted Delaware's Constitution of 1776. Following the capture of President John McKinly in Wilmington and his narrow escape from Philadelphia, Read returned home and took the office of President. During the occupation of Philadelphia from 1777 to 1778, Read worked to recruit soldiers to protect Delaware. The assembly was moved to Dover. Ceasar Rodney succeeded Read as President of Delaware but Read continued to serve in the legislature through 1788.

In 1786, Read represented Delaware at the Annapolis Convention, the precursor to the Constitutional Convention. He then represented Delaware in Philadelphia the next year. Read was an early proponent of a strong central government. He was for the abolition of the individual states, but with little support, shifted to policies that protected the smaller states. Said one of the delegates of Read, "his legal abilities are said to be very great, but his powers of oratory are fatiguing and tiresome to the last degree; his voice is feeble and his articulation so bad that few can have patience to attend him." Nevertheless, Delaware was the first state to ratify the Constitution, in large part thanks to Read.

Following the U.S. Constitution's ratification, Read was elected one of the first two senators from Delaware, serving from 1789 until he resigned in 1793 to become Chief Justice of the Delaware Supreme Court.

George Read died at his home in New Castle, Delaware, on September 21, 1798, and is buried at the Immanuel Episcopal Church Cemetery, nearby. His gravestone reads, "Member of the Congress of the Revolution, The Convention that framed the Constitution of the U.S. and of the first Senate under it. Judge of Admiralty, President and Chief Justice of Delaware and A signer of the Declaration of Independence."

Regarding the family legacy, brother Thomas Read was an officer in the Continental Navy during the Revolution. Another brother, James, was an officer in the Continental Army and was later active in managing the navy under the Articles of Confederation. George Read's son George Read Jr. served as the first U.S. Attorney for Delaware and his grandson George Read III served as the second. Another son, John, was a noted lawyer and banker of Philadelphia. George Read's great-granddaughter, Louisa, married Maj. Benjamin Kendrick Pierce, the brother of future President Franklin Pierce.

Caesar Rodney
(1728 – 1784)

Rode for Independence

Buried at Christ Episcopal Church Cemetery (cenotaph?),
Dover, Delaware.

––––•–•–•––––

**Continental Association • Declaration of Independence
Military**

Caesar Rodney was a militia commander in the American Revolutionary
War, a delegate from Delaware in both the First and Second Continental
Congress, and a signer of the Declaration of Independence. He is most
famous for riding on horseback for 70 miles through a storm to reach
the Pennsylvania State House in time to cast the decisive Delaware vote
for independence.

––––◆◇◆––––

Rodney was born on his father's large and prosperous farm near
Dover, Delaware on October 7, 1728. The farm became known as
"Byfield" and was worked by many slaves. At the age of seventeen, his
father died and guardianship was entrusted to a man named Nicholas
Ridgely. Rodney received very little formal education. He was tormented
throughout his life by asthma, and his adult years were plagued by facial
cancer. He experienced expensive, painful, and futile medical treatments.
He would often wear a green scarf to hide his disfigured face. The disease
would eventually kill him.

He lived all his life as a bachelor and was known for his wit and
humor and was very popular. He served in the Delaware Militia during

Portrait of Caesar Rodney, artist unknown.

the French and Indian War where he was commissioned a captain and in 1755 was elected Sheriff of Kent County and served the maximum three years allowed. This was a powerful position in that it supervised elections and chose the grand jurors that set the county tax rate. After his term as Sheriff, he served in a variety of government offices in Delaware. He became prominent in what was known as the Country Party and as a result, worked closely with Thomas McKean.

He began his service in the Delaware Assembly in 1762 and continued in office through 1776. Several times he served as speaker including on June 15, 1776, when the Assembly of Delaware voted to sever all ties with the British Parliament and King.

He and McKean were elected to the Stamp Act Congress in 1765 and Rodney was the leader of the Delaware Committee of Correspondence formed to communicate with other colonies. In 1769, he tried unsuccessfully to have a law passed "prohibiting the importation of slaves" into Delaware. In 1766 he was named to the Supreme Court of the colony even though he served in the Assembly. Meanwhile, Rodney served in the Continental Congress along with McKean and George Read from 1774 through 1776. As a member of the First and Second Continental Congress, he listened intently to the debates on independence without committing himself. He even signed the Olive Branch Petition seeking reconciliation with England in 1775, but was finally convinced that Britain "was making every kind of exertion in her favor to reduce us to unconditional submission and that no hope of reconciliation on constitutional principles could possibly remain."

The busy Rodney was appointed a colonel in May of 1775 and in September of that same year he became a brigadier general and later a major general. He served in the New Jersey area during this time and was responsible for producing the required Delaware troops to General George Washington. As a member of the Council of Safety, he was unable to secure the timely response to troop equipment needs and bought the necessary items from his own pocket. This effort resulted in many letters from Washington lauding his work.

The Continental Congress met in the spring and summer of 1776 to contemplate declaring independence from the British Crown. The Delaware delegates were Rodney, McKean, and Read. The awesome consequences of this to the country as a whole, and to the lives and fortunes of these delegates can hardly be overstated. The discussion of the resolution made by Richard Henry Lee of Virginia took several contentious weeks. Unanimous agreement eluded its supporters and a recess was declared. The Congress reconvened on July 1. Rodney, however, was in Sussex County to look into a threatened Loyalist uprising. He received word from McKean via courier that the vote on independence was the next day and that he and George Read were deadlocked. He immediately left for Philadelphia. It was an agonizing eighty-mile ride through the summer's heat, an angry thunderstorm, and torrential rain, over dirt roads choked with mud, across rickety bridges spanning swollen streams, and over slippery cobblestone streets of the towns. He was a lone rider with no time to spare. All that he had worked for hung in the balance. He rushed to

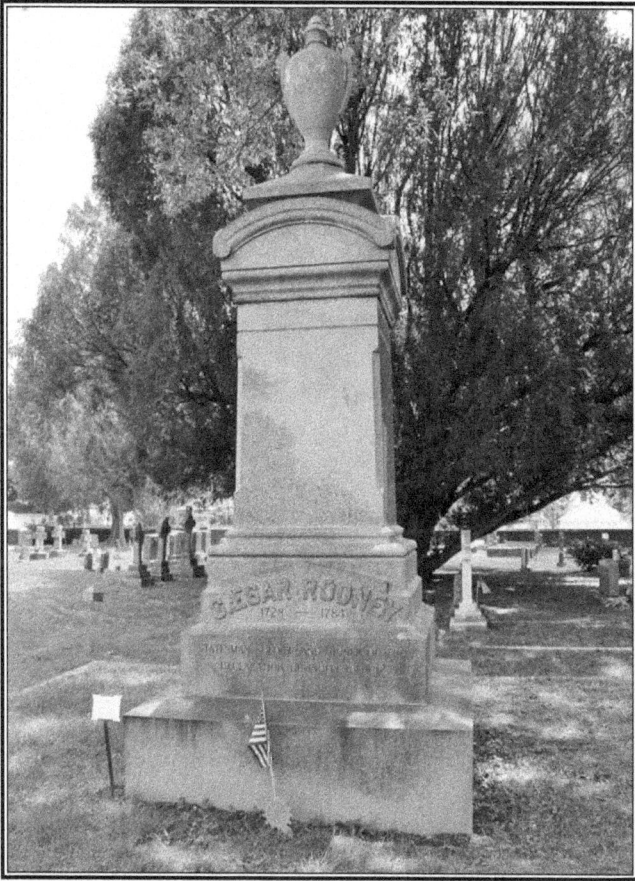

Grave of Caesar Rodney at Christ Episcopal Church Cemetery in Dover, Delaware (photo by Lawrence Knorr).

vote for a resolution that might put a noose around his neck. He arrived "in his boots and spurs" just as the voting was beginning. He voted with McKean and thereby allowed Delaware to join eleven other states in voting for independence. The wording of the Declaration of Independence was approved two days later and Rodney signed it on August 2.

In 1777 Rodney was placed in charge of the post at Trenton. He was to forward troops from Trenton to Morristown as fast as possible. On February 18 of that year, Washington wrote a letter of commendation to Rodney for the job he did in Trenton. In March 1778 he was elected as the President of Delaware, an office he served until November

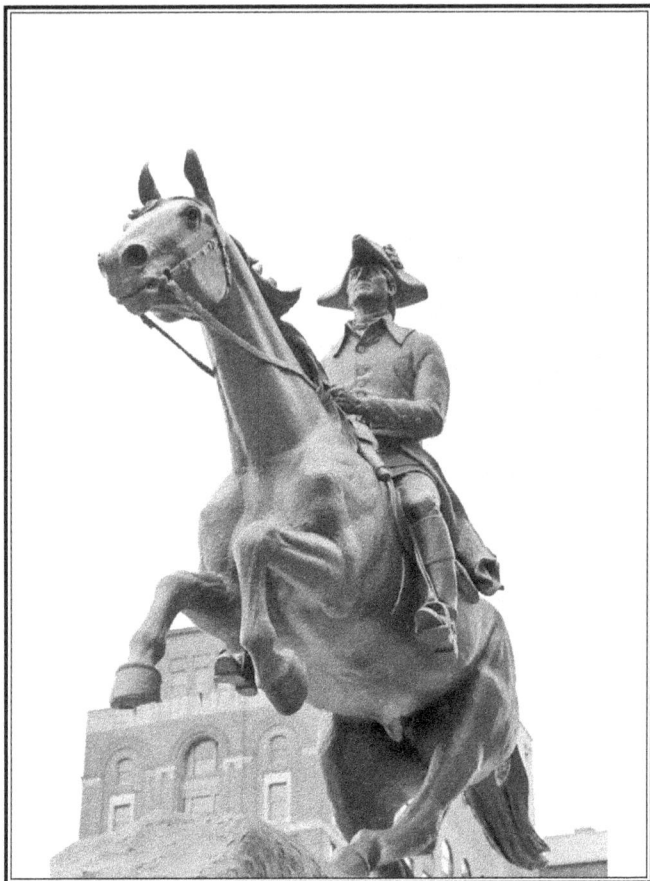

Equestrian statue of Caesar Rodney at Rodney Square in Wilmington, Delaware (photo by Lawrence Knorr).

1781. During this time there was real contention over the ratification of the Articles of Confederation which consumed his energy. He was again elected to the Continental Congress in 1782 and 1783 but was unable to serve because of his poor health. In the fall of 1783 despite his poor condition, he was elected the Speaker of the Delaware General Assembly. He served as best he could but by the early spring of 1784, he became too weak to travel. The upper assembly voted to hold future meetings at Rodney's home, which they did for the next few weeks.

Caesar Rodney died at age fifty-six at his home near Dover on June 26, 1784, and was buried at "Poplar Grove," his home on the "Byfield" plantation. Rodney's will provided for the emancipation of his slaves. His grave, for some reason, went unmarked for over a hundred years. There are different opinions about where Rodney is buried. Some believe that in 1888, Rodney's remains were moved to Christ Episcopal Churchyard and an impressive twelve-foot granite monument was erected at this site by the National Sons of The American Revolution. Some believe that the remains moved weren't those of Caesar but of a relative. In Washington, D.C., near the Washington Monument, there is a memorial park and lagoon honoring the signers of the Declaration of Independence, and a granite block there bears the name of Caesar Rodney. There is also a statue of Rodney in Statuary Hall in the U.S. Capitol and a large equestrian statue, memorializing his famous ride, looms over Rodney Square in downtown Wilmington, Delaware.

Nicholas Van Dyke
(1738 – 1789)

President of Delaware

Buried at Immanuel Episcopal Churchyard,
New Castle, Delaware.

Articles of Confederation

Colonial America politically and economically was dominated by the more populous areas that made up Massachusetts, Pennsylvania, and Virginia. During these times, the inhabitants of the smaller colonies looked to their leaders to protect their interests during the formation of the American nation. The small state of Delaware was represented by well-known patriots like Caesar Rodney, John Dickinson, and some lesser-known but just as able men. One of these lesser-knowns was Nicholas Van Dyke.

Van Dyke was born on September 25, 1738, in New Castle County near the present site of Delaware City. As a youth, he was educated at home before studying law in Philadelphia where he was admitted to the Pennsylvania Bar in1765. He then returned to New Castle where he began a law practice and married. His first wife died bearing the couple's first child in 1767. He remarried and had four additional children. One of his children would become a United States Senator and one grandchild a Congressman.

Showing an interest in the politics of the day, Van Dyke sided with the colonies in their conflicts with English rule. He was elected

Nicholas Van Dyke (1738–1789)

Old postcard of Amstel House in New Castle, Delaware, the former home of Nicholas Van Dyke.

to Delaware's Boston Relief Committee in 1774 and, though viewed as a more conservative voice than that of Caesar Rodney, he still enjoyed the confidence of his fellow citizens as evidenced by his service at the Delaware Constitutional Convention of 1776. During the convention, Van Dyke worked closely with George Read, a signer of the Declaration of Independence, and those efforts gained him Read's lasting respect and admiration. He served in the state council at the same time and was appointed as Judge of Delaware's Admiralty Court.

In 1777 Van Dyke was elected to the Continental Congress replacing John Evans who declined to serve. While serving in Congress, he signed the Articles of Confederation. He did so despite his disagreement with the provision that permitted unlimited territorial expansion to the west for those states that had western frontiers. Van Dyke believed that these lands should be shared by all of the states in the Confederation.

In 1782 John Dickinson resigned as President (the equivalent of our current governors) of Delaware. The Delaware General Assembly voted to choose a successor. Van Dyke received 18 of the 30 votes cast and won the election. It's been said that one of his proudest moments while holding this office came on June 5, 1783, when he happily announced to the Assembly that the Treaty of Paris officially ending the Revolutionary War had been signed.

During his term as President of Delaware, Van Dyke's daughter married. Among the many friends who made the trip to attend the wedding was none other than George Washington. It is said that Washington enjoyed himself at the celebration so much that in addition to kissing the bride he made a point of kissing all the pretty women that had gathered at Van Dyke's home after the ceremony.

Van Dyke was President of Delaware at a time when he had to deal with Delaware's Revolutionary War debt. He devised a plan and successfully implemented the process by which his state paid off their portion of that debt. He also had to deal with the fate of a British loyalist named Cheney Chow. Chow had been tried on the charge of treason and

The worn tombstone of Nicholas Van Dyke at Immanuel Episcopal Churchyard, New Castle, Delaware.

acquitted but he was also charged with killing a member of the posse that had been sent to arrest him. Though the evidence against him was flimsy at best, Chow was convicted and sentenced to death in May of 1783. Van Dyke felt that pardoning Chow would destroy his political career but at the same time he was aware that many prominent citizens, including Caesar Rodney's brother Thomas, considered the condemned man innocent. Van Dyke handled the situation by postponing the execution indefinitely.

After the end of his term as Delaware's President in 1786, Van Dyke resumed his law practice. He passed away on one of his farms on February 18, 1789, and was buried in a family plot on the property. His remains were later moved to the Immanuel Episcopal Church Cemetery in New Castle. Van Dyke's son Nicholas, Jr., represented Delaware in both the United States House of Representatives and the Senate. One of his grandsons Kensey Johns Jr. served in the U. S. House.

Sources

Books, Magazines, Journals, Files:

Appleby, Joyce. *Inheriting the Revolution: The First Generation of Americans.* Cambridge, Massachusetts: Harvard University Press, 2000.

Atkinson, Rick. *The British Are Coming: The War for America, Lexington to Princeton, 1775-1777.* New York: Henry Holt & Co. 2019.

Bordewich, Fergus M. *The First Congress: How James Madison, George Washington, and a Group of Extraordinary Men Invented the Government.* New York: Simon and Schuster Paperbacks, 2016.

Boudreau, George W. *Independence: A Guide to Historic Philadelphia.* Yardley, Pennsylvania: Westholme Publishing, LLC. 2012.

Bowen, Catherine Drinker. *Miracle at Philadelphia: The Story of the Constitutional Convention May to September 1787.* Boston, Massachusetts: Little, Brown & Company, 1966.

Breen, T.H, *George Washington's Journey: The President Forges a New Nation.* New York: Simon & Schuster. 2016.

Chambers, II, John Whiteclay. *The Oxford Companion to American Military History.* Oxford: Oxford University Press, 1999.

Commager, Henry Steele & Richard B. Morris. *The Spirit of 'Seventy-Six: The Story of the American Revolution as Told by Participants.* New York: Harper & Rowe, 1967.

Conlin, Joseph R. *The Morrow Book of Quotations in American History.* New York: William Morrow and Company, Inc., 1984.

Daniels, Jonathan. *Ordeal of Ambition.* Garden City, New York: Doubleday & Company, Inc., 1970.

Dann, John C. *The Revolution Remembered: Eyewitness Accounts of the War for Independence.* Chicago: University of Chicago Press, 1980.

DeRose, Chris. *Founding Rivals: Madison vs. Monroe: The Bill of Rights and the Election that Saved a Nation.* New York: MJF Books, 2011.

Drury, Bob & Tom Clavin. *Valley Forge.* New York: Simon & Schuster. 2018.

Ellis, Joseph J. *Revolutionary Summer: The Birth of American Independence.* New York: Alfred A. Knopf, 2013.

———. *The Quartet: Orchestrating the Second American Revolution, 1783-1789.* New York: Alfred A. Knopf, 2015.

———. *His Excellency: George Washington.* New York: Alfred A. Knopf, 2004.

Flexner, James Thomas. *George Washington in the American Revolution, 1775-1783.* Boston: Little, Brown & Company, 1967.

Goodrich, Charles A. *Lives of the Signers of the Declaration of Independence.* Charlotteville, N.Y.: SamHar Press, 1976.

SOURCES

Grossman, Mark. *Encyclopedia of the Continental Congress*. Armenia, New York: Grey House Publishing, 2015.

Kiernan, Denise & Joseph D'Agnese. *Signing Their Lives Away: The Fame and Misfortune of the Men Who Signed the Declaration of Independence*. Philadelphia: Quirk Books, 2008.

———. *Signing Their Rights Away: The Fame and Misfortune of the Men Who Signed the United States Constitution*. Philadelphia: Quirk Books, 2011.

Klarman, Michael J. *The Framers' Coup: The Making of the United States Constitution*. New York: Oxford University Press, 2016.

Langguth, A. J. *Patriots*. New York: Simon and Schuster, 1988.

Larson, Edward J. *A Magnificient Catastrophe*. New York: Free Press, 2007.

Lee, Mike. *Written Out of History: The Forgotten Founders Who Fought Big Government*. New York: Penguin Books, 2017.

Lomask, Milton. *Charles Carroll and the American Revolution*. San Francisco: Ignatius Press, 2017.

Lossing, Benson J. *Pictorial Field Book of the Revolution*. New York: Harper Brothers. 1851.

Maier, Pauline. *American Scripture: Making the Declaration of Independence*. New York: Alfred A. Knopf, Inc., 1997.

Middlekauff, Robert. *The Glorious Cause: The American Revolution, 1763-1789*. Oxford: Oxford University Press, 2005.

Miller, Jr., Arthur P. & Marjorie L. Miller. *Pennsylvania Battlefields and Military Landmarks*. Mechanicsburg, Pennsylvania: Stackpole Books, 2000.

Millett, Allan R. & Peter Maslowski. *For the Common Defense: A Military History of the United States of America*. New York: The Free Press, 1984.

O'Connell, Robert L. *Revolutionary: George Washington at War*. New York: Random House. 2019.

Racove, Jack N. *Revolutionaries: A New History of the Invention of America*. New York: Houghton Mifflin Harcourt, 2011.

Raphael, Ray. *Founding Myths: Stories That Hide Our Patriotic Past*. New York: MJF Books, 2004.

Rossiter, Clinton. *1787 The Grand Convention*. New York: The Macmillan Company, 1966.

Schweikart, Larry & Michael Allen. *A Patriot's History of the United States from Columbus's Great Discovery to the War on Terror*. New York: Penguin, 2004.

Sharp, Arthur G. *Not Your Father's Founders*. Avon, Massachusetts: Adams Media, 2012.

Taafee, Stephen R. *The Philadelphia Campaign, 1777-1778*. Lawrence, Kansas: University of Kansas Press, 2003.

Wood, Gordon S. *The Radicalism of the American Revolution*. New York: Vintage Books, 1993.

———. *Empire of Liberty: A History of the Early Republic, 1789-1815*. New York: Penguin Books, 2004.

———. *Revolutionary Characters: What Made the Founders Different*. New York: Penguin Books, 2006.

———. *The Americanization of Benjamin Franklin*. Oxford: Oxford University Press, 2009.

Wright, Benjamin F. *The Federalist: The Famous Papers on the Principles of American Government: Alexander Hamilton, James Madison, John Jay*. New York: Metro Books, 2002.

Video Resources:

Guelzo, Allen C. *The Great Courses: America's Founding Fathers (Course N. 8525)*. Chantilly, Virginia: The Teaching Company, 2017.

Online Resources:

Archives.gov – for information on the Constitutional Convention.

CauseofLiberty.blogspot.com – for information on Daniel Carroll.

ColonialHall.com – for information about the signers of the Declaration of Independence.

DSDI1776.com – for information on many Founders.

FamousAmericans.net – for information on many Founders.

FindaGrave.com – for burial information, vital statistics and obituaries.

FirstLadies.org – for information on Abigail Adams.

Newspapers.com – Hundreds of newspaper articles were accessed—too numerous to mention here.

NPS.gov – for information on various park sites.

TheHistoryJunkie.com – for information on multiple Founders.

USHistory.org – for information on multiple Founders.

Wikipedia.com – for general historical information.

Index

www.ingramcontent.com/pod-product-compliance
Lightning Source LLC
Chambersburg PA
CBHW022346040426
42449CB00006B/741